Grade 1

Carson-Dellosa Publishing LLC
Greensboro, North Carolina

Credits
Author: Chandler Tyrrell
Copy Editor: Angela Triplett

Visit *carsondellosa.com* for correlations to Common Core, state, national, and Canadian provincial standards.

Carson-Dellosa Publishing LLC
PO Box 35665
Greensboro, NC 27425 USA
carsondellosa.com

ISBN 978-1-4838-5015-3
01-312181151

Table of Contents

Introduction

Problem Solving 4 Today: Daily Skill Practice is a comprehensive yet quick and easy-to-use supplement to any classroom math curriculum. This series will strengthen students' problem-solving skills as they review and use strategies to solve word problems in numbers, operations, algebraic thinking, measurement, data, and geometry.

This book covers 40 weeks of daily problem-solving practice. Essential problem-solving skills are practiced each day during a four-day period with a problem-solving strategy introduced at the beginning of each week. Students are encouraged to solve the problems each day using the specified strategy. On the fifth day, an assessment is given to allow students to prove their competency in using the weekly strategy. Although the strategies are presented in a consecutive format, they can be used in any order.

Various problem-solving skills and strategies are reinforced throughout the book through activities that align to state standards. To view these standards, see the Standards Alignment Chart on page 7.

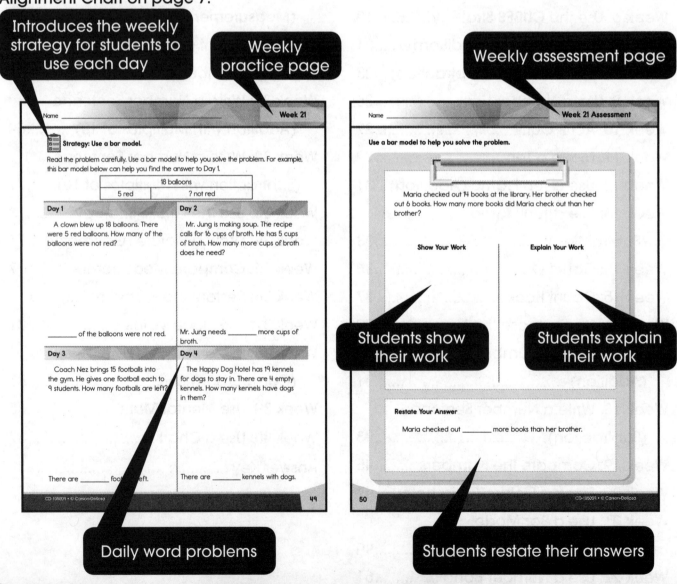

Introduces the weekly strategy for students to use each day

Weekly practice page

Weekly assessment page

Students show their work

Students explain their work

Daily word problems

Students restate their answers

Developing Problem-Solving Skills

Solving word problems is an essential skill that every student must master. Developing and practicing problem-solving strategies enables students to deal more effectively and successfully with most types of mathematical problems.

With this series, a word problem will be presented each day for students to solve using a strategy that is intended to work well with the problem. Teachers should review and discuss the strategy and its applications at the beginning of each week. The word problems can then be given as part of a morning work routine, given as a nightly homework assignment, used in math journals, or cut apart and placed in a math center. The weekly assessment page is useful to have students show the steps they took to solve the word problem and to explain their reasoning.

The Problem-Solving Process

When solving math problems, students should be encouraged to follow this general problem-solving process as well as to develop and use their own problem-solving strategies.

Understand
- Restate the problem in your own words.
- What facts/information/data are given?
- What are you being asked to find?
- What information is missing or not needed?

Plan
- Which strategy should I use?
- Have I solved similar problems before?

Act
- Implement a strategy.
- Check each step of the plan as you work it.

Reflect
- Have you answered the question?
- Is the answer reasonable and accurate?
- Can you find another method or work backward to check your work?

Tracking Problem-Solving Skills

Have students use the reproducible on page 6 to keep track of their understanding of solving word problems. Four times during the year, have students complete the first column by adding the date and then drawing the appropriate symbol for each I Can . . . statement using the key under the chart. Repeat several times to show progress throughout the year. Have students answer the prompts at the bottom of the page to assess their overall learning.

Name _____

Word Problems

Skill	Date	Date	Date	Date
I can choose the correct operation.				
I can identify key words.				
I can use a drawing.				
I can use a number sentence.				
I can explain my answer.				
I can solve addition word problems.				
I can solve subtraction word problems.				
I can solve word problems involving measurement.				
I can solve word problems involving shapes.				

Ratings	✗ = not yet	? = maybe	✓ = yes

One thing I understand well is

One thing I can improve on is

Standards Alignment Chart

State Standards*		Weeks
Operations and Algebraic Thinking		
Represent and solve problems involving addition and subtraction.	1.OA.1, 1.OA.2	1–18, 21, 22, 24, 28, 33, 38
Understand and apply properties of operations and the relationship between addition and subtraction.	1.OA.3, 1.OA.4	6, 11, 13, 15, 16, 24, 28
Add and subtract within 20.	1.OA.5, 1.OA.6	1–18, 21, 22, 24, 28, 33, 38
Work with addition and subtraction equations.	1.OA.7, 1.OA.8	1–18, 21, 22, 24, 33, 38
Numbers and Operations in Base Ten		
Extend the counting sequence.	1.NBT.1	26, 30, 31, 33, 36
Understand place value.	1.NBT.2, 1.NBT.3	19, 25, 27, 31–33, 37, 39
Use place value understanding and properties of operations to add and subtract.	1.NBT.4–1.NBT.6	21, 23, 25, 26, 27, 30–33, 36, 39
Measurement and Data		
Measure lengths indirectly and by iterating length units.	1.MD.1, 1.MD.2	29, 35
Represent and interpret data.	1.MD.4	40
Geometry		
Reason with shapes and their attributes.	1.G.1–1.G.3	20, 34

The research is clear that family involvement is strongly linked to student success. Support for student learning at home improves student achievement in school. Educators should not underestimate the significance of this connection.

The skill-building format of this book creates an opportunity to expand this school-to-home connection. Students are encouraged to practice their word problem-solving skills at home. Parents and guardians can use the reproducible strategy sheet (below) to help their students solve word problems at home during the week. The CUBES chart can also be used in the classroom by posting it in a math center or allowing students to glue it into their math journals.

In order to make the school-to-home connection successful for students and their families, it may be helpful to reach out to them with an introductory letter. Explain the problem-solving process and the CUBES strategy. Encourage them to offer suggestions or feedback along the way.

CUBES

Problem-Solving Strategy

C — Circle the numbers.

U — Underline the question.

B — Box the key words.

E — Eliminate extra information.
Evaluate: What steps do I take?

S — Solve and check.

Strategy: Circle the important numbers.

Read the problem carefully. Circle the numbers you will use to help you solve the problem. Day 1 has been started for you.

Day 1	Day 2
In Jon's driveway, there is a bike with ②tires. There is also a car with ④tires. How many tires are in the driveway in all?	Bill has 3 pets. Holly has 2 pets. How many pets do Bill and Holly have in all?
There are _____ tires in the driveway.	They have _____ pets in all.

Day 3	Day 4
Hanna has 8 markers. Her friend gives her 2 more. How many markers does Hanna have now?	There are 7 pencils in a box. Mr. Nelson adds 2 more pencils to the box. How many pencils are there in the box now?
Hanna has _____ markers.	There are _____ pencils in the box.

Circle the important numbers to help you solve the problem.

There were 5 fish in the water. Soon, 5 more fish came to join them. How many fish were there altogether?

Show Your Work	Explain Your Work

Restate Your Answer

There were _____ fish in the water altogether.

Strategy: Underline the question.

Read the problem carefully. What do you need to find? Underline the question in the problem. Then, you can be sure your solution answers it. Day 1 has been started for you.

Day 1	Day 2
Jill picked 4 flowers. Her dad gave her 5 more. <u>How many flowers does Jill have in all?</u>	Mr. Quan has 9 rosebushes and 3 trees to trim. How many more rosebushes does Mr. Quan have to trim than trees?
Jill has _____ flowers in all.	Mr. Quan has to trim _____ more rosebushes.
Day 3	**Day 4**
Lyla has 2 toy cars and 6 toy trucks. How many toy cars and trucks does she have altogether?	Lee has 4 ribbons. Kayla has 3 more ribbons than Lee. How many ribbons does Kayla have?
Lyla has _____ toy cars and trucks.	Kayla has _____ ribbons.

Underline the question to help you solve the problem.

Mrs. Ross bought 10 bagels. The clerk put them into 2 bags. She has 4 bagels in one bag. How many bagels are in the other bag?

Show Your Work

Explain Your Work

Restate Your Answer

There are _____ bagels in the other bag.

Strategy: Box the key words.

Read the problem carefully. Draw a box around the word or words that tell you whether to add or subtract to help you solve the problem. Day 1 has been started for you.

Day 1	Day 2
Nell has 6 ⬜fewer⬜ books than Luke. Luke has 13 books. How many books does Nell have?	Max has 10 more markers than Kit. Kit has 8 markers. How many markers does Max have?
Nell has _____ books.	Max has _____ markers.

Day 3	Day 4
Greg has 4 erasers. His friend gives him 3 more erasers. How many erasers does Greg have now?	Jamie went fishing with his dad. He caught 9 fish the first day. The second day, he caught 13 fish. How many more fish did he catch on the second day?
Greg has _____ erasers now.	Jamie caught _____ more fish on the second day.

Box the key words to help you solve the problem.

A gardener planted 12 trees in one row. She planted 7 trees in another row. How many trees did she plant altogether?

Show Your Work | **Explain Your Work**

Restate Your Answer

The gardener planted _____ trees altogether.

Strategy: Evaluate and eliminate information.

Read the problem carefully. Look closely at the information you have been given. Cross out any information that is not needed for solving the problem. Day 1 has been started for you.

Day 1	Day 2
Ruby has 4 pillows on her bed. Sam has 5 pillows on her bed. ~~Ruby also has 3 stuffed animals on her bed.~~ How many pillows do the girls have in all?	Tara has 10 hairclips and 6 hairbows. Reba has 2 more hairclips than Tara. How many hairclips does Reba have?

Ruby and Sam have _____ pillows in all.

Reba has _____ hairclips.

Day 3	Day 4
Mr. Vale and Mr. Ito are friends. Mr. Vale has 4 children. Mr. Ito has 7 children. How many fewer children does Mr. Vale have than Mr. Ito?	Marcus is 8 years old. He is in third grade. His little sister, Mia, is 3 years old. She is in preschool. How many years older is Marcus than his sister?

Mr. Vale has _____ fewer children than Mr. Ito.

Marcus is _____ years older than Mia.

Cross out the information that is not needed to help you solve the problem.

Hong has 16 large rubber bands. He has 9 small rubber bands. Most of the rubber bands are green. How many more large rubber bands does Hong have than small rubber bands?

Show Your Work	**Explain Your Work**

Restate Your Answer

Hong has _____ more large rubber bands.

Strategy: Solve and check.

After you have solved the problem, check your answer. Have you answered the question that was asked? Does your answer make sense?

Day 1

Penny puts her dolls on 2 shelves. The top shelf has 4 dolls. If she has 9 dolls in all, how many are on the bottom shelf?

There are _____ dolls on the bottom shelf.

Day 2

Owen has 5 fewer pieces of gum in his bag than Pablo. Pablo has 12 pieces of gum. How many pieces of gum does Owen have?

Owen has _____ pieces of gum.

Day 3

There were 8 lights on in the house. Ms. Park turned off 3 lights. How many lights are still on in the house?

There are _____ lights still on.

Day 4

Quinn picked 8 apples. Rick picked 5 apples. How many apples did both boys pick in all?

Quinn and Rick picked _____ apples.

Use the solve-and-check strategy to help you solve the problem.

Finn counted 5 black cars and 6 white cars in the parking lot. How many black and white cars did Finn count in all?

Show Your Work	**Explain Your Work**

Restate Your Answer

Finn counted _____ black and white cars.

Strategy: Use the CUBES strategy.

Circle important numbers. **U**nderline the question. **B**ox the key words. **E**valuate and eliminate extra information. **S**olve and check.

Day 1	Day 2
Taylor wrote 12 emails on Monday. He wrote 6 emails on Tuesday. He used his mom's computer. How many emails did Taylor write on Monday and Tuesday in all?	Mr. Nez read 6 fewer magazines than Ms. Jung. Ms. Jung read 9 magazines and 3 books. How many magazines did Mr. Nez read?
Taylor wrote _____ emails in all.	Mr. Nez read _____ magazines.

Day 3	Day 4
Tatum is 7 years old. She has 3 fewer bracelets than her sister. Her sister has 17 bracelets. How many bracelets does Tatum have?	There are 19 seahorses swimming in a reef. Some of the seahorses leave to find food. Now, there are 12 seahorses swimming in the reef. How many seahorses are left?
Tatum has _____ bracelets.	There are _____ seahorses left.

Use the CUBES strategy to help you solve the problem.

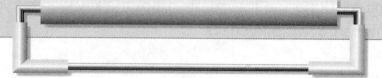

Raven pours 16 cups of lemonade for a party. She has invited 15 people to the party. At the party, 13 people each drink a cup of lemonade. How many cups of lemonade are left over?

Show Your Work | **Explain Your Work**

Restate Your Answer

There are _____ cups of lemonade left over.

Strategy: Draw a picture.

Read the problem carefully. Draw a picture that will help you solve the problem.

Day 1	Day 2
Zoe collected bugs. She counted 5 bugs in one jar. She counted 9 bugs in a second jar. Then, she let all of the bugs go. How many bugs did Zoe collect in all?	Colin counts 8 raisins in his cereal. His sister counts 7 raisins in her cereal. How many raisins do they count altogether?
Zoe collected _____ bugs.	They count _____ raisins altogether.

Day 3	Day 4
There are 8 ladybugs on a flower. Then, 8 more ladybugs join them. How many ladybugs are on the flower now?	There are 3 flowers on a bush on Monday. On Tuesday, 9 more flowers bloom. How many flowers are on the bush now?
There are _____ ladybugs on the flower.	There are _____ flowers on the bush.

Draw a picture to help you solve the problem.

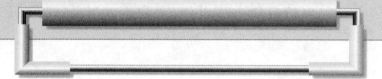

Ben has 12 plants. He puts them into 2 window boxes. He puts 8 plants in one window box. How many plants does Ben put in the other window box?

Show Your Work	**Explain Your Work**

Restate Your Answer

Ben puts _____ plants in the other window box.

Strategy: Draw a picture.

Read the problem carefully. Draw a picture that will help you solve the problem.

Day 1	Day 2
There are 13 dragonflies near a pond. Then, 9 dragonflies fly away. How many dragonflies are still left near the pond?	There are 10 berries in a bowl. Angela eats some of the berries. Now, there are 5 berries in the bowl. How many berries did Angela eat?
There are _____ dragonflies left near the pond.	Angela ate _____ berries.
Day 3	**Day 4**
Paige has 13 dolls. She gives 3 dolls to her friend. How many dolls does Paige have left?	Jay has 16 marbles. He gives 5 marbles to his friend. How many marbles does Jay have left?
Paige has _____ dolls left.	Jay has _____ marbles left.

Draw a picture to help you solve the problem.

Penny has 11 ribbons. Mona has 5 fewer ribbons than Penny. How many ribbons does Mona have?

Show Your Work | **Explain Your Work**

Restate Your Answer

Mona has _____ ribbons.

Strategy: Use a number line.

Read the problem carefully. Use the number line to help you solve the problem.

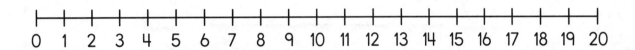

| Day 1 | Day 2 |

Day 1

A fish tank holds 12 fish. Mr. Conti adds 3 more fish. How many fish are in the tank now?

There are _____ fish in the tank now.

Day 2

Kade has 13 stickers. He gives his friend 5 of the stickers. How many stickers does Kade have left?

Kade has _____ stickers left.

Day 3

There are 8 boys and 11 girls in Ms. Chu's class. How many students total are there in Ms. Chu's class?

There are _____ students in Ms. Chu's class.

Day 4

Uri bought some stamps. He bought 15 animal stamps and 4 sports stamps. How many stamps did Uri buy in all?

Uri bought _____ stamps in all.

Use the number line to help you solve the problem.

Ling ran for 17 minutes on Friday morning. In the afternoon, he ran for 5 minutes. How many more minutes did Ling run in the morning?

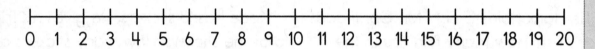

Show Your Work	**Explain Your Work**

Restate Your Answer

Ling ran for _____ more minutes in the morning.

Strategy: Act it out.

Read the problem carefully. Act out the problem with objects or people to help you solve the problem.

Day 1	Day 2
Ms. Peters puts 6 bracelets on one arm. She puts 11 bracelets on the other arm. How many bracelets is she wearing in all?	Elle jumps 4 times. Then, she jumps 13 more times. How many times did Elle jump in all?
Ms. Peters is wearing _____ bracelets.	Elle jumped _____ times.

Day 3	Day 4
Ross laid 12 coins in a row. Then he added 4 more coins to the row. How many coins are in the row now?	Ginny counted 12 teachers on the playground. Then, she saw 3 teachers take their classes inside. How many teachers were left on the playground?
There are _____ coins in the row now.	Ginny saw _____ teachers left on the playground.

Act it out to help you solve the problem.

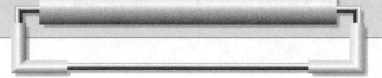

Gavin cleaned out his desk. He took out 4 markers from his desk. Then, he got 10 pencils out. Last, he took 3 books from his desk. How many items did Gavin take out of his desk in all?

Show Your Work | **Explain Your Work**

Restate Your Answer

Gavin took _____ items out of his desk.

Strategy: Make a ten.

Read the problem carefully. Look for number pairs that add up to 10. Then, add the third number to 10.

Day 1

A frog caught 2 dragonflies, 8 spiders, and 3 ladybugs. How many insects did the frog catch?

The frog caught _____ insects.

Day 2

Drew picked up 9 oak leaves, 5 maple leaves, and 1 elm leaf. How many leaves did Drew pick up altogether?

Drew picked up _____ leaves altogether.

Day 3

Anya did 5 push-ups. Colin did 5 push-ups. Derek did 4 push-ups. How many push-ups did the three children do altogether?

The three children did _____ push-ups altogether.

Day 4

Josie has 4 books about cats. She has 8 books about dogs. She has 6 books about horses. How many books does Josie have in all?

Josie has _____ books in all.

Make a ten first to help you solve the problem.

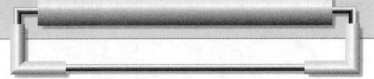

Mr. Ahmed's class is having a food drive. Travis brought in 3 cans of food. Lee brought in 4 cans. Liza brought in 7 cans. How many cans of food did the three students bring in all?

Show Your Work	**Explain Your Work**

Restate Your Answer

The three students brought in _____ cans of food.

Strategy: Use a ten frame.

Read the problem carefully. Use a ten frame to help you solve the problem.

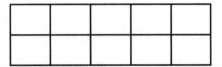

Day 1

Blair has 5 red bows and 5 yellow bows. How many bows does she have in all?

Blair has _____ bows in all.

Day 2

Anton saw 3 elephants at the zoo. He saw 7 monkeys. How many elephants and monkeys did Anton see?

Anton saw _____ monkeys and elephants.

Day 3

Ivan made 3 paper snowflakes. His little sister made 4 paper snowflakes. How many total snowflakes did Ivan and his sister make?

They made _____ snowflakes.

Day 4

Liv made 2 phone calls on Friday. She made 3 more phone calls on Saturday. On Sunday, she made 4 phone calls. How many phone calls did she make in all?

Liv made _____ phone calls in all.

Use a ten frame to help you solve the problem.

Drake rode his bike to John's house. Drake rode past 3 houses. He turned the corner. Then, he rode past 6 more houses. How many houses in all did Drake pass?

Show Your Work	**Explain Your Work**

Restate Your Answer

Drake passed _____ houses in all.

Strategy: Use a ten frame.

Read the problem carefully. Use a ten frame to help you solve the problem.

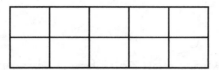

Day 1

Harry has 10 almonds. He gives 7 almonds to his brother. How many almonds does Harry have left?

Harry has _____ almonds left.

Day 2

Ms. Walsh has 2 plates. She puts 10 orange slices on the plates. If she puts 5 slices on one plate, how many are on the other plate?

There are _____ slices on the other plate.

Day 3

A group of 10 students stands in 2 lines. The first line has 6 students. How many students are in the second line?

There are _____ students in the second line.

Day 4

Yuri found 10 shells on the beach. He chose 8 shells to take home. How many shells did he leave behind?

Yuri left behind _____ shells.

Draw a ten frame to help you solve the problem.

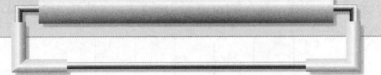

Tia downloaded 10 songs on her phone. Her brother downloaded 4 songs on his computer. How many more songs did Tia download than her brother?

Show Your Work	Explain Your Work

Restate Your Answer

Tia downloaded _____ more songs than her brother.

Strategy: Count on.

Read the problem carefully. Count on to help you solve the problem.

Day 1	**Day 2**

Day 1

Raul painted 15 stars. Then, he painted 3 more stars. How many stars did he paint altogether?

Raul painted _____ stars altogether.

Day 2

Mr. Wolf pulled 12 carrots from his garden. Then, he pulled 5 radishes. How many carrots and radishes did Mr. Wolf pull from his garden in all?

Mr. Wolf pulled _____ carrots and radishes from his garden in all.

Day 3

Mrs. Gladd planted 11 bushes on Saturday. She planted 4 more bushes on Sunday. How many bushes did Mrs. Gladd plant?

Mrs. Gladd planted _____ bushes.

Day 4

Jamal read 10 pages of his book in the morning. In the afternoon, he read another 7 pages. How many total pages did Jamal read?

Jamal read _____ total pages.

Count on to help you solve the problem.

Noah ate 16 cherries for a snack. Then, he ate 5 grapes. How many cherries and grapes did Noah eat in all?

Show Your Work	**Explain Your Work**

Restate Your Answer

Noah ate _____ cherries and grapes in all.

Strategy: Count back.

Read the problem carefully. Count back to help you solve the problem.

Day 1	Day 2
Philip has 15 marbles. He gives 4 marbles to Harper. How many marbles does Philip have now?	Mrs. Diaz has 12 rings in a jewelry box. She puts on 3 of the rings. How many rings are left in the jewelry box?
Philip has _____ marbles now.	There are _____ rings left in the jewelry box.
Day 3	**Day 4**
There were 19 sheep grazing on a hill. Then, 4 sheep walked away. How many sheep are on the hill now?	Tanner took a test. It had a total of 20 questions. Tanner got 2 answers wrong. How many answers did Tanner get right?
There are _____ sheep on the hill.	Tanner got _____ answers right.

Count back to help you solve the problem.

Jada and her mother counted 18 weeds in the garden. Jada pulled up 5 of the weeds. Her mother pulled up the other weeds. How many weeds did Jada's mother pull up?

Show Your Work	Explain Your Work

Restate Your Answer

Jada's mother pulled up _____ weeds.

Strategy: Decompose the numbers.

Read the problem carefully. Think about how a number can be made up of smaller parts. For example, 5 can be made up of 4 + 1 or 2 + 3. Decompose the numbers to help you solve the problem.

Day 1	Day 2
Shane has 7 erasers. Some are pink. Some are white. How many of each color does Shane have? Write 2 possible answers.	There are 9 birds in a tree. Some are robins. Some are bluebirds. How many of each bird are there? Write 2 possible answers.

_____ pink and _____ white

_____ pink and _____ white

_____ robins and _____ bluebirds

_____ robins and _____ bluebirds

Day 3	Day 4
Tracy has 8 shirts and dresses. How many of each does she have? Write 2 possible answers.	There are 6 daisies and tulips in a vase. How many of each flower are there? Write 2 possible answers.

_____ shirts and _____ dresses

_____ shirts and _____ dresses

_____ daisies and _____ tulips

_____ daisies and _____ tulips

Decompose numbers to help you solve the problem.

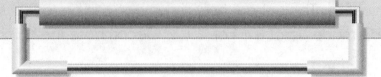

Tara has 10 bracelets and necklaces. How many of each does she have? Write 2 possible answers.

Show Your Work | **Explain Your Work**

Restate Your Answer

_____ bracelets and _____ necklaces

_____ bracelets and _____ necklaces

Strategy: Write a number sentence.

Read the problem carefully. Write a number sentence that you can use to help you solve the problem. Day 1 has been started for you.

Day 1	Day 2
One frog caught 8 flies. Another frog caught 7 flies. How many flies did the two frogs catch in all?	Daysha put 8 cans and 9 bottles into the recycling bin. How many items in all did Daysha put into the bin?

_____7_____ + _____8_____ = _____

The frogs caught _____flies.

Daysha put _____ items in the bin.

Day 3	Day 4
A dog had 5 brown puppies and 7 black puppies. How many puppies were there in all?	Chang has 14 baseball cards. Tomás has 3 baseball cards. How many cards do the boys have in all?

There were _____ puppies.

The boys have _____ baseball cards in all.

Write a number sentence to help you solve the problem.

On Monday, Viv drank 6 glasses of water. On Tuesday, she drank 7 glasses of water. How many glasses of water did she drink altogether on the two days?

Show Your Work

Explain Your Work

Restate Your Answer

Viv drank _____ glasses of water on the two days.

Strategy: Write a number sentence.

Read the problem carefully. Write a number sentence that you can use to help you solve the problem. Day 1 has been started for you.

Day 1	Day 2
The pet store had 15 guinea pigs for sale. They sold 4 guinea pigs. How many guinea pigs were still for sale?	Grandma sewed 12 doll dresses. She gave Ruby 4 of the dresses. How many doll dresses does Grandma still have?

Day 1

The pet store had 15 guinea pigs for sale. They sold 4 guinea pigs. How many guinea pigs were still for sale?

_____ – _____ = _____

There were _____ guinea pigs still for sale.

Day 2

Grandma sewed 12 doll dresses. She gave Ruby 4 of the dresses. How many doll dresses does Grandma still have?

Grandma still has _____ doll dresses.

Day 3

Mr. Beck brought 18 muffins to the market. He sold 9 of them. How many muffins did Mr. Beck have left?

Mr. Beck had _____ muffins left.

Day 4

There were 14 toys on Gene's bedroom floor. He picked up 6 of the toys. How many toys were still on the floor?

There were _____ toys left on the floor.

Write a number sentence to help you solve the problem.

Tasha had 19 paper clips in her backpack. She used 7 paper clips during class. How many paper clips did Tasha have left?

Show Your Work	Explain Your Work

Restate Your Answer

Tasha had _____ paper clips left.

Strategy: Compare the numbers.

Read the problem carefully. Use what you know about tens and ones to help you solve the problem.

Day 1

Sara and Sam are at the store. They see 27 red umbrellas and 25 yellow umbrellas. Sara says there are more red umbrellas. Sam says there are more yellow umbrellas. Who is right? How do you know?

_____ is right. There are more _____ umbrellas.

Day 2

Mr. Brown counted 31 cars and 13 trucks in his parking garage. Did he count more cars or trucks? How do you know?

Mr. Brown counted more _____ .
I know because _____ is more than _____ .

Day 3

At the Slippery Seal Swim School, 18 swimmers are boys. There are 28 girls. Ana says there are more girls. Ben says there are more boys. Who is right? How do you know?

_____ is right. There are more _____ .

Day 4

Brady counts his beads. He has 27 red beads, 37 green beads, and 17 blue beads. He needs to put them in order from the least to greatest amounts. How should he do it?

Compare numbers to help you solve the problem.

Alex put 37 glow-in-the-dark stars on the wall. She put 27 stars on the ceiling. Did Alex put more stars on the wall or on the ceiling?

Show Your Work	**Explain Your Work**

Restate Your Answer

Alex put more stars on the _____ .

CD-105009 • © Carson-Dellosa

Strategy: Draw a picture.

Read the problem carefully. Draw a picture to help you solve the problem.

Day 1	Day 2
David is in a school play about shapes. His costume is a closed shape with 4 sides. All 4 sides are the same length. Draw the shape of David's costume.	Grace got a new hat for her birthday. The hat is a closed shape with 3 sides. Draw the shape of Grace's hat.

Day 3	Day 4
Nora's rug is shaped like a rectangle. It also has 2 rectangle shapes on it. Draw what you think Nora's rug looks like.	Max drew a square with a triangle on top of it. He thinks it looks like the shape of a house. Draw what you think Max's shapes look like.

Draw a picture to help you solve the problem.

Orlando's shirt has a red shape on the front of it. The shape has 4 angles and 4 sides. It is not a square or rectangle. Draw the shape that could be on Orlando's shirt.

Show Your Work   **Explain Your Work**

Restate Your Answer

A _____ could be on the front of Orlando's shirt.

Strategy: Use a bar model.

Read the problem carefully. Use a bar model to help you solve the problem. For example, this bar model can help you find the answer to Day 1.

18 balloons	
5 red	? not red

Day 1

A clown blew up 18 balloons. There were 5 red balloons. How many of the balloons were not red?

_____ of the balloons were not red.

Day 2

Mr. Jung is making soup. The recipe calls for 16 cups of broth. He has 5 cups of broth. How many more cups of broth does he need?

Mr. Jung needs _____ more cups of broth.

Day 3

Coach Nez brings 15 footballs into the gym. He gives one football each to 9 students. How many footballs are left?

There are _____ footballs left.

Day 4

The Happy Dog Hotel has 19 kennels for dogs to stay in. There are 4 empty kennels. How many kennels have dogs in them?

There are _____ kennels with dogs.

Use a bar model to help you solve the problem.

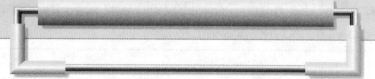

Maria checked out 14 books at the library. Her brother checked out 6 books. How many more books did Maria check out than her brother?

| **Show Your Work** | **Explain Your Work** |

Restate Your Answer

Maria checked out _____ more books than her brother.

Strategy: Use a number bond.

Read the problem carefully. Use a number bond to help you solve the problem. For example, this number bond can help you find the answer to Day 1.

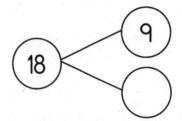

Day 1

Nina has 18 blocks. She has 9 red blocks. The rest of the blocks are blue. How many blue blocks does she have?

Nina has _____ blue blocks.

Day 2

There are 12 stalls in the barn. There are horses in 9 of the stalls. How many stalls are empty?

There are _____ empty stalls.

Day 3

Ace has 13 marbles. Bo has 6 marbles. How many marbles do the boys have altogether?

The boys have _____ marbles altogether.

Day 4

Jay exercised for 15 minutes. He ran for 8 minutes. The rest of the time he lifted weights. How long did Jay lift weights?

Jay lifted weights for _____ minutes.

Use a number bond to help you solve the problem.

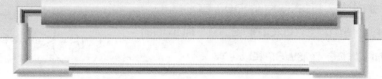

There are 14 pencils in a box. Mai takes 9 pencils from the box. She gives them to her friends. How many pencils are left in the box?

Show Your Work	**Explain Your Work**

Restate Your Answer

There are _____ pencils left in the box.

Strategy: Use a chart.

Read the problem carefully. Use a hundred chart to help you solve the problem.

Day 1	Day 2
There are 32 students on the bus. At the next stop, 10 more students get on the bus. How many students are on the bus now?	Charlie has 54 toy cars. His friend gives him 20 more. How many cars does he have now?
There are _____ on the bus now.	Charlie has _____ cars now.
Day 3	**Day 4**
Jon counts 70 ants crawling on a picnic blanket. Then, 20 more ants join them. How many ants are on the blanket now?	Colin walked for 33 minutes in the morning. He walked for 30 more minutes in the afternoon. How many minutes did he walk altogether?
There are _____ ants on the blanket.	Colin walked _____ minutes altogether.

Use a hundred chart to help you solve the problem.

The penguins at the zoo ate 22 fish in the morning. They ate 30 fish in the afternoon. How many fish did the penguins eat in all?

Show Your Work	**Explain Your Work**

Restate Your Answer

The penguins ate _____ fish in all.

Strategy: Use a number line.

Read the problem carefully. Use the number line to help you solve the problem.

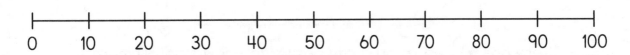

| | | | | | | | | | | |
|0|10|20|30|40|50|60|70|80|90|100|

Day 1

Tony collects trading cards. He has 10 cards to start with. His dad gives him 20 more. How many trading cards does Tony have now?

Tony has _____ trading cards now.

Day 2

Sienna read 10 pages in her book last night. This morning she read 10 more pages. How many pages did she read in all?

Sienna read _____ pages in her book in all.

Day 3

The school store has 60 pencils. The principal bought 20 more pencils for the store. How many pencils does the school store have now?

The store has _____ pencils now.

Day 4

The school cafeteria workers fixed 40 cheese sandwiches and 30 ham sandwiches for lunch. How many sandwiches did they fix altogether?

The cafeteria fixed _____ sandwiches altogether.

Use the number line to help you solve the problem.

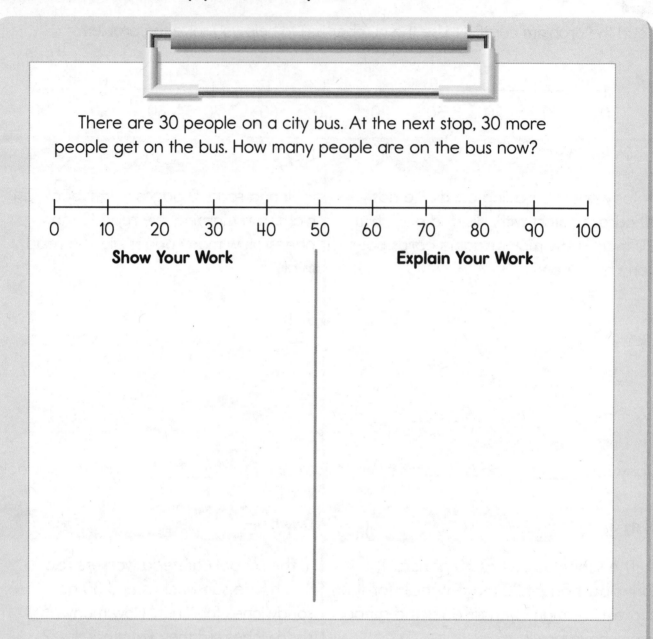

There are 30 people on a city bus. At the next stop, 30 more people get on the bus. How many people are on the bus now?

0   10   20   30   40   50   60   70   80   90   100

Show Your Work   **Explain Your Work**

Restate Your Answer

There are _____ people on the bus now.

Strategy: Use a number line.

Read the problem carefully. Use the number line to help you solve the problem.

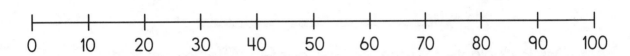

0	10	20	30	40	50	60	70	80	90	100

Day 1

At a pet store, there are 60 fish in a tank. Someone buys 10 fish. How many fish are left in the tank?

There are _____ fish left in the tank.

Day 2

Jamal has 80 sheets of paper. He uses 10 sheets for drawing. How many sheets of paper does he have now?

Jamal has _____ sheets of paper left now.

Day 3

There are 40 students on the playground. Then, 20 students go inside. How many students are still on the playground?

There are _____ students still on the playground.

Day 4

Leah has 70 red beads. She uses 20 red beads to make a bracelet. How many red beads does she have left?

Leah has _____ red beads left.

Use the number line to help you solve the problem.

Ms. Park planted 90 seeds in her garden. After one month, 30 seeds have sprouted. How many seeds have not yet sprouted?

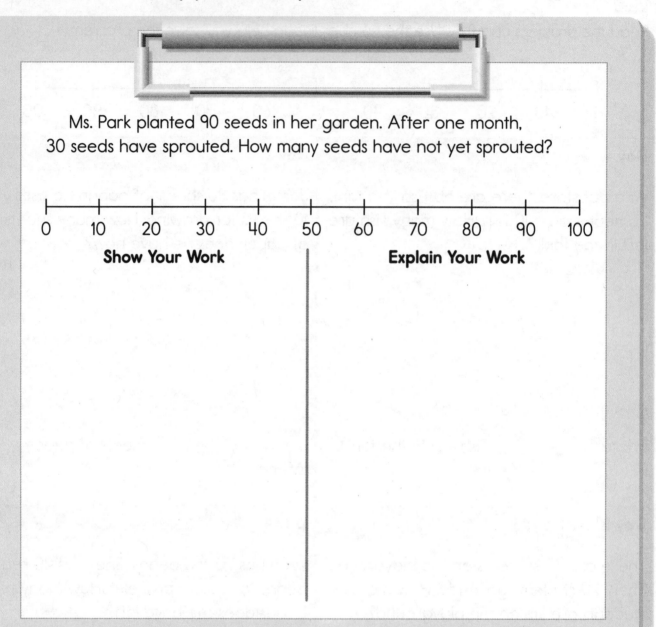

0   10   20   30   40   50   60   70   80   90   100

Show Your Work   **Explain Your Work**

Restate Your Answer

There are _____ seeds that have not yet sprouted.

Strategy: Use a model.

Read the problem carefully. Use counters, base ten blocks, or linking cubes to help you solve the problem.

Day 1	Day 2
Quinten inflates 14 blue balloons. He inflates 5 red balloons. How many balloons in all has he inflated?	Bill sells 21 newspapers one day. He sells 6 more the next day. How many newspapers has he sold in all?
Quinten has inflated _____ balloons.	Bill has sold _____ newspapers in all.
Day 3	**Day 4**
Grace swam for 18 minutes. Then, she swam for 7 minutes more. How many total minutes did Grace swim?	Ryan saw 17 birds on a hike. He saw 5 squirrels. How many birds and squirrels did Ryan see on his hike in all?
Grace swam for _____ total minutes.	Ryan saw _____ birds and squirrels on his hike in all.

Use a model to help you solve the problem.

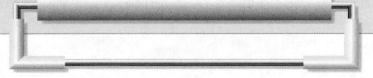

A first grade class at Elm Elementary School found 20 cans and 7 bottles for a recycling project. How many cans and bottles did the class find in all?

| **Show Your Work** | **Explain Your Work** |

Restate Your Answer

The class found _____ cans and bottles in all.

Strategy: Use a symbol.

Read the problem carefully. Write a number sentence to help you solve. Use a symbol for the number you do not know. For example, 10 + 3 + **?** = 20 can help you solve Day 1.

Day 1	Day 2
Lana counts 20 red, yellow, and blue pencils in a cup. She counts 10 red pencils. She counts 3 yellow pencils. How many blue pencils did she count?	Ian collected a total of 18 shells on Friday, Saturday, and Sunday. He collected 4 shells on Friday. He collected 8 shells on Saturday. How many shells did he collect on Sunday?
Lana counted _____ blue pencils.	Ian collected _____ shells on Sunday.

Day 3	Day 4
There are some dogs at the dog park. There are 2 black dogs and 9 spotted dogs. There are 5 white dogs. How many dogs are at the dog park in all?	Holly counted 15 goats at the petting zoo. There were 5 white goats and 3 gray goats. The rest were black. How many goats were black?
There are _____ dogs at the park in all.	There were _____ black goats at the petting zoo.

Use a symbol for the unknown to help you solve the problem.

Maya made a fruit salad. She added 19 berries. She put in 4 blueberries and 5 blackberries. Then, she added some strawberries. How many strawberries did she add to the fruit salad?

Show Your Work	**Explain Your Work**

Restate Your Answer

Maya put _____ strawberries in the fruit salad.

Strategy: Write a number sentence.

Read the problem carefully. There are two steps to solving it. Write an addition number sentence and a subtraction number sentence to help you solve the problem.

Day 1	Day 2
On vacation, Hector took 5 pictures at a zoo and 10 pictures at a museum. Later, he deleted 8 of the pictures. How many pictures did he have left?	Trinity picked 4 tulips and 10 roses to make a flower bouquet for her mother. She only used 9 of the flowers. How many extra flowers did she pick?
Hector had _____ pictures left.	Trinity picked _____ extra flowers.

Day 3	Day 4
Harry wanted to start a video game collection. He bought 6 games from a friend and bought 7 more at a garage sale. If 3 of the games didn't work, how many working games did he buy?	Taylor had 14 math problems and 4 reading problems for homework. She only finished 8 of the problems before dinner. How many more problems did she have left to finish?
Harry bought _____ working games.	Taylor had _____ problems left to finish.

Write two number sentences to help you solve the problem.

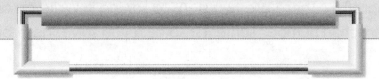

Megan bought some new and used books at a book fair. She bought 13 fiction books and 5 nonfiction books. If 4 of the books were new, how many were used?

Show Your Work

Explain Your Work

Restate Your Answer

Megan bought _____ used books.

Strategy: Use a model.

Read the problem carefully. Use the model to help you solve the problem.

Day 1	**Day 2**

Day 1

Dawn measured the pencil using linking cubes. How many cubes long is the pencil?

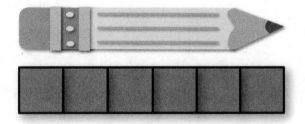

The pencil is _____ linking cubes long.

Day 2

Will measured the comb on his dresser using paper clips. How many paper clips long is Will's comb?

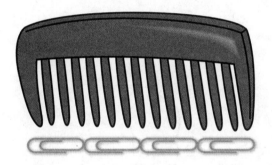

The comb is _____ paper clips long.

Day 3

Tom measured his fishing pole with the fish that he caught. How many fish are equal to the length of his fishing pole?

The fishing pole is _____ fish long.

Day 4

Danny's father asked him to measure how long his screwdriver was. Danny did not have a ruler, so he measured it using paper clips. How many paper clips long was the screwdriver?

The screwdriver is _____ paper clips long.

Use linking cubes as a model to help you solve the problem.

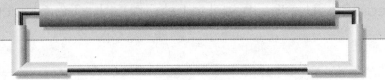

Mia pulled a carrot from her garden. She measured it using linking cubes. About how many linking cubes tall was her carrot?

Show Your Work	Explain Your Work

Restate Your Answer

The carrot was about _____ linking cubes tall.

Strategy: Count on or count back.

Read the problem carefully. Decide if it is an addition problem or a subtraction problem. Count on or count back to help you solve the problem.

Day 1	Day 2
There are 32 people on the bus. The bus stops, and 4 more people get on. How many people are on the bus now?	There are 25 baseballs in a supply closet. The coach takes 5 of the baseballs out for practice. How many baseballs are left in the closet now?

There are _____ people on the bus now.

There are _____ baseballs left in the closet.

Day 3	Day 4
Sasha has already read 51 pages of her book. She reads another 6 pages after lunch. How many pages has Sasha read of her book?	Devin has 43 pennies in a plastic bag. The bag has a hole in it and 4 pennies fall out. How many pennies does Devin have in the bag now?

Sasha has read _____ pages of her book.

Devin has _____ pennies in the bag now.

Count on to help you solve the problem.

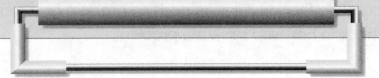

There are 48 geese swimming in the pond. Another 6 geese land in the water. How many geese are swimming in the pond now?

Show Your Work	**Explain Your Work**

Restate Your Answer

There are _____ geese swimming in the pond now.

Name _____

 Strategy: Write a number sentence.

Read the problem carefully. Write a number sentence to help you solve the problem.

Day 1	Day 2
Carly spent 15 minutes doing her math homework. She spent 10 minutes doing her reading homework. How much time did Carly spend doing her homework?	Ms. Nichols put 34 children on one bus for a field trip. She put 30 children on another bus. How many children are on the two buses altogether?

Carly spent _____ minutes doing homework.

There are _____ children on the two buses altogether.

Day 3	Day 4
Sam has 30 rocks in his collection. He adds 8 more rocks to the collection. How many rocks does Sam have now?	Ms. Yu sees 21 ducks swimming in a pond. She watches as 10 more ducks join them. How many ducks are swimming in the pond now?

Sam has _____ rocks now.

There are _____ ducks swimming in the pond now.

Write a number sentence to help you solve the problem.

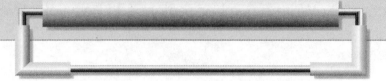

Tad has scored 30 points in his new video game. He needs 20 more points to get to the next level. How many points does it take in all to get to the next level?

Show Your Work

Explain Your Work

Restate Your Answer

Tad needs _____ points in all to get to the next level.

Strategy: Write a number sentence.

Read the problem carefully. Write a number sentence to help you solve the problem.

Day 1	Day 2
There were 40 beetles under a log. A hiker picked up the log and 20 beetles crawled away. How many beetles were left under the log?	Avery has 50 coins in her coin collection. When she moved, Avery lost 20 coins. How many coins does she have in her collection now?
There are _____ beetles under the log now.	Avery has _____ coins in her collection.

Day 3	Day 4
Mrs. Silva made 70 bracelets for the craft fair. She sold 50 of the bracelets. How many bracelets does Mrs. Silva have left over?	Drake collected 80 buttons to recycle. He used 30 buttons for an art project. How many buttons does Drake have left?
Mrs. Silva has _____ bracelets left over.	Drake has _____ buttons left.

Write a number sentence to help you solve the problem.

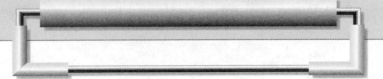

Jasmin counted 90 pennies in her piggy bank. She bought a piece of ribbon with 20 pennies. How many pennies does Jasmin have left in her piggy bank?

Show Your Work

Explain Your Work

Restate Your Answer

Jasmin has _____ pennies left in her piggy bank.

Name _____

 Strategy: Use the CUBES strategy.

Circle important numbers. **U**nderline the question. **B**ox the key words. **E**valuate and eliminate extra information. **S**olve and check.

Day 1	Day 2

Day 1

   Beth collects 26 oak leaves, 20 maple leaves, and 15 acorns. How many total leaves does Beth collect?

Beth collects _____ total leaves.

Day 2

   Fiona has 3 sisters. Her sister Ellen is 12 years old. Her sister Ivy is 8. Fiona is 6. How much older is Ellen than Fiona?

Ellen is _____ years older than Fiona.

Day 3

   Jack has 40 red beads in a jar. He also has 7 green beads that are not in a jar. How many beads does Jack have in all?

Jack has _____ beads in all.

Day 4

   As Ingrid walks, she counts her steps. When she reaches 90 steps, she stops. Then, she takes another 9 steps. How many steps has she taken altogether?

Ingrid has taken _____ steps altogether.

Use the CUBES strategy to help you solve the problem.

There are 6 players on the blue team. There are 10 players on the red team. Each team needs to have the same number of players. How many players need to leave the red team and join the blue team?

Show Your Work	**Explain Your Work**

Restate Your Answer

There are _____ players that need to leave the red team and join the blue team.

Strategy: Draw a picture.

Read the problem carefully. Draw a picture to help you solve the problem.

Day 1	Day 2
Cara drew a circle. Then, she added a line that divided the circle in half. Show what Cara drew.	Davis and Eric share a piece of paper shaped like a rectangle. They cut it into 2 equal pieces. Show at least 2 ways they could have divided the paper.

Day 3	Day 4
Ms. Dumon sliced a round pizza into 4 equal pieces. Show how Ms. Dumon sliced the pizza.	Chris used a triangle and one other shape to make a pentagon. Draw the other shape that Chris could have used to make a pentagon.

Draw a picture to help you solve the problem.

Mr. Garcia wants to cut a square piece of wood into 2 pieces. He wants the pieces to be the same size. He also wants them to be shaped like triangles. Lee says that it cannot be done. Mark says it can. Who is right?

Show Your Work	**Explain Your Work**

Restate Your Answer

_____ is right. It _____ be done.

Strategy: Compare measurements.

Read the problem carefully. Compare the measurements to help you solve the problem.

Day 1	Day 2
Ms. Brenner asked 3 boys to line up from shortest to tallest. Ray is taller than either Quan or Trent. Trent is taller than Quan. List the boys in order from shortest to tallest.	Lori sees 3 trees at a park. The oak tree is taller than the elm tree. A maple tree is shorter than the elm tree. List the trees Lori saw in order from shortest to tallest.

_____ , _____ , _____   _____ , _____ , _____

Day 3	Day 4
Rick's pencil is shorter than Simone's pencil. Simone's pencil is shorter than Rachel's pencil. Which student has the longest pencil?	Ty needs to use the shortest scissors he can to cut his art project. He sees red scissors that are longer than blue scissors. He sees green scissors that are shorter than the blue scissors. Which color of scissors should he use?

The student with the longest pencil is

_____ .

Ty should use the _____ scissors.

Compare measurements help you solve the problem.

Jorge uses a penny to measure the first piece of string. It is 4 pennies long. Jorge uses a pencil to measure the second piece of string. It is 4 pencils long. Is the first piece of string longer or the second piece? How do you know?

Show Your Work	Explain Your Work

Restate Your Answer

The _____ piece of string is longer.

I know because _____

_____ .

Strategy: Restate the problem.

Read the problem carefully. Restate the problem in your own words to help you solve the problem.

Day 1

Lynn bought 7 pencils, 8 erasers, and 2 books at the school book fair. How many items did Lynn buy in all?

Lynn bought _____ items in all.

Day 2

Seth walks dogs for his neighbors. On Mondays, he walks 12 dogs. On Tuesdays, he walks 16 dogs. How many more dogs does Seth walk on Tuesdays?

Seth walks _____ more dogs on Tuesdays.

Day 3

There are 14 turtles on a rock. Some of the turtles crawl into the water. Now there are 9 turtles on the rock. How many turtles crawled into the water?

There are _____ turtles that crawled into the water.

Day 4

A bowl holds 12 pieces of fruit. There are 4 bananas, 3 apples, and some oranges. How many oranges are in the bowl?

There are _____ oranges in the bowl.

Restate the problem in your own words to help you solve the problem.

David's class had earned 10 points for good behavior. They need 30 points to get a pizza party on Friday. How many more points do they need to have the party?

Show Your Work

Explain Your Work

Restate Your Answer

David's class needs _____ more points to have the party.

Strategy: Use place value.

Read the problem carefully. Use what you know about place value to help you solve the problem.

Day 1

There are 7 fish tanks at the pet store. Each tank has 10 fish in it. In the eighth tank, there are 4 fish. How many fish are there in all 8 tanks?

There are _____ fish in all.

Day 2

There are 3 vans with 10 students in each van. A fourth van has 8 students. How many students are riding in the vans in all?

There are _____ students in the vans in all.

Day 3

Mr. Ortiz has 5 new packs of gum. Each new pack has 10 pieces of gum. Mr. Ortiz also has an opened pack. It has 7 pieces in it. How many pieces of gum does Mr. Ortiz have in all?

Mr. Ortiz has _____ pieces of gum in all.

Day 4

Each row in a parking lot has 10 spaces for cars. There are 6 rows with no empty spaces left. The seventh row has 4 cars parked in it. How many parked cars are in the 7 rows altogether?

There are _____ parked cars altogether.

Use place value to help you solve the problem.

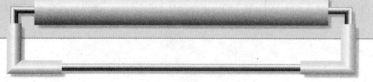

Lily is packing books in boxes. She can fit 10 books in each box. She has 77 books. She fills 7 boxes with books. How many books are left?

Show Your Work

Explain Your Work

Restate Your Answer

There are _____ books left.

Strategy: Use a bar model.

Read the problem carefully. Use a bar model to help you find the answer. For example, the bar model can help you find the answer to Day 1.

Bill	7	
Alexa	3	
Hector	3	3	= ?

Day 1

Bill has 7 pens. Alexa has 3 pens. Hector has twice as many pens as Alexa. Who has more pens, Bill or Hector?

_____ has more pens than

_____ .

Day 2

There are 5 sheep. There are 8 ducks. There are twice as many chickens as sheep. Are there more ducks or chickens?

There are more _____ .

Day 3

Julio ran for 6 minutes. Irene ran twice as long as Julio. Kaylen ran for 13 minutes. Who ran for more minutes, Kaylen or Irene?

_____ ran for more

minutes than _____ .

Day 4

The florist has 10 roses. She has half as many tulips as roses. She has 4 daisies. Are there more tulips or daisies?

There are more _____ .

Use a bar model to help you solve the problem.

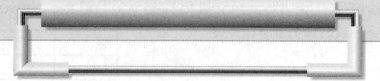

Lamar has 18 red marbles. He has 8 green marbles. He has twice as many yellow marbles as green marbles. Does Lamar have more red marbles or more yellow marbles?

Show Your Work

Explain Your Work

Restate Your Answer

Lamar has more _____ marbles.

Strategy: Use mental math.

Read the problem carefully. Use mental math to help you solve the problem. Remember to check your answer to make sure it makes sense.

Day 1

Kami and Heath are playing a game. Kami has 53 points. Heath has 10 more points than Kami. How many points does Heath have?

Heath has _____ points.

Day 2

Jared has 75 arcade tickets. He gives 10 of the tickets to a friend. How many tickets does he have now?

Jared has _____ tickets.

Day 3

Paige got 22 text messages in the morning. She got 10 more texts later that day. How many texts did she get in all?

Paige got _____ text messages in all.

Day 4

There are 27 carrots growing in the garden. Ms. Valdez pulls up 10 carrots. How many carrots are left in the garden?

There are _____ carrots in the garden.

Use mental math to help you solve the problem.

Henry owns a pet-sitting business. During one month, he takes care of 20 cats and 10 dogs. He also takes care of 10 birds. How many animals does Henry take care of during one month?

Show Your Work	**Explain Your Work**

Restate Your Answer

Henry cares for _____ animals during one month.

Strategy: Use a chart.

Read the problem carefully. Use the chart to help you solve the problem.

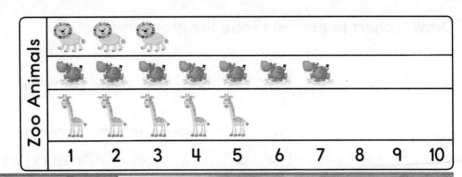

Day 1

Paul made a chart to show how many of each animal he saw at the zoo. How many different kinds of animals are in Paul's chart?

There are _____ different kinds of animals in the chart.

Day 2

How many more giraffes did Paul see than lions?

Paul saw _____ more giraffes than lions.

Day 3

How many more hippos did Paul see than lions?

Paul saw _____ more hippos than lions.

Day 4

Paul told his mother that he saw 16 animals at the zoo in all. Is he correct?

Paul _____ correct. He saw _____ animals at the zoo.

Draw a chart to help you solve the problem.

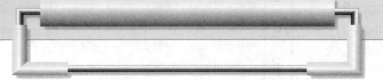

Monique has 3 different colors of markers in her desk. She wants to use a chart to show how many markers she has in each color. She has 8 red markers, 5 green markers, and 4 blue markers. Draw a chart that shows how many of each color she has. How many total markers does Monique have?

Show Your Work	**Explain Your Work**

Restate Your Answer

Monique has _____ markers.

Answer Key

Page 9
Check students' work. **Day 1:** 6; **Day 2:** 5;
Day 3: 10; **Day 4:** 9

Page 10
Check students' work and reasoning. 10

Page 11
Check students' work. **Day 1:** 9; **Day 2:** 6;
Day 3: 8; **Day 4:** 7

Page 12
Check students' work and reasoning. 6

Page 13
Check students' work. **Day 1:** 7; **Day 2:** 18;
Day 3: 7; **Day 4:** 4

Page 14
Check students' work and reasoning. 19

Page 15
Check students' work. **Day 1:** 9; **Day 2:** 12;
Day 3: 3; **Day 4:** 5

Page 16
Check students' work and reasoning. 7

Page 17
Check students' work. **Day 1:** 5; **Day 2:** 7;
Day 3: 5; **Day 4:** 13

Page 18
Check students' work and reasoning. 11

Page 19
Check students' work. **Day 1:** 18; **Day 2:** 3;
Day 3: 14; **Day 4:** 7

Page 20
Check students' work and reasoning. 3

Page 21
Check students' work. **Day 1:** 14; **Day 2:** 15;
Day 3: 16; **Day 4:** 12

Page 22
Check students' work and reasoning. 4

Page 23
Day 1: 4; **Day 2:** 5; **Day 3:** 10; **Day 4:** 11

Page 24
Check students' work and reasoning. 6

Page 25
Check students' work. **Day 1:** 15; **Day 2:** 8;
Day 3: 19; **Day 4:** 19

Page 26
Check students' work and reasoning. 12

Page 27
Check students' work. **Day 1:** 17; **Day 2:** 17;
Day 3: 16; **Day 4:** 9

Page 28
Check students' work and reasoning. 17

Answer Key

Page 29
Check students' work. **Day 1:** 13; **Day 2:** 15;
Day 3: 14; **Day 4:** 18

Page 30
Check students' work and reasoning. 14

Page 31
Check students' work. **Day 1:** 10; **Day 2:** 10;
Day 3: 7; **Day 4:** 9

Page 32
Check students' work and reasoning. 9

Page 33
Check students' work. **Day 1:** 3; **Day 2:** 5;
Day 3: 4; **Day 4:** 2

Page 34
Check students' work and reasoning. 6

Page 35
Check students' work. **Day 1:** 18; **Day 2:** 17;
Day 3: 15; **Day 4:** 17

Page 36
Check students' work and reasoning. 21

Page 37
Check students' work. **Day 1:** 11; **Day 2:** 9;
Day 3: 15; **Day 4:** 18

Page 38
Check students' work and reasoning. 13

Page 39
Check students' work. **Days 1–4:** Answers
will vary.

Page 40
Check students' work and reasoning.
Answers will vary.

Page 41
Check students' work. **Day 1:** 8 + 7 = 15;
Day 2: 8 + 9 = 17; **Day 3:** 5 + 7 = 12;
Day 4: 14 + 3 = 17

Page 42
Check students' work and reasoning.
6 + 7 = 13

Page 43
Check students' work. **Day 1:** 15 – 4 = 11;
Day 2: 12 – 4 = 8; **Day 3:** 18 – 9 = 9;
Day 4: 14 – 6 = 8

Page 44
Check students' work and reasoning.
19 – 7 = 12

Page 45
Check students' work. **Day 1:** Sara, red;
Day 2: cars, 31 is more than 13; **Day 3:** Ana,
girls; **Day 4:** 17, 27, 37

Page 46
Check students' work and reasoning. wall

Answer Key

Page 47
Check students' work. **Day 1:** square; **Day 2:** triangle; **Day 3:** rectangle with two smaller rectangles inside it; **Day 4:** square with a triangle on top

Page 48
Check students' work and reasoning. Drawings will vary but should show a quadrilateral that is neither a square nor a rectangle.

Page 49
Check students' work. **Day 1:** 13; **Day 2:** 11; **Day 3:** 6; **Day 4:** 15

Page 50
Check students' work and reasoning. 8

Page 51
Check students' work. **Day 1:** 9; **Day 2:** 3; **Day 3:** 19; **Day 4:** 7

Page 52
Check students' work and reasoning. 5

Page 53
Check students' work. **Day 1:** 42; **Day 2:** 74; **Day 3:** 90; **Day 4:** 63

Page 54
Check students' work and reasoning. 52

Page 55
Check students' work. **Day 1:** 30; **Day 2:** 20; **Day 3:** 80; **Day 4:** 70

Page 56
Check students' work and reasoning. 60

Page 57
Check students' work. **Day 1:** 50; **Day 2:** 70; **Day 3:** 20; **Day 4:** 50

Page 58
Check students' work and reasoning. 60

Page 59
Check students' work. **Day 1:** 19; **Day 2:** 27; **Day 3:** 25; **Day 4:** 22

Page 60
Check students' work and reasoning. 27

Page 61
Check students' work. **Day 1:** 7; **Day 2:** 6; **Day 3:** 16; **Day 4:** 7

Page 62
Check students' work and reasoning. 10

Page 63
Check students' work. **Day 1:** 7; **Day 2:** 5; **Day 3:** 10; **Day 4:** 10

Page 64
Check students' work and reasoning. 14

Page 65
Check students' work. **Day 1:** 6; **Day 2:** 4; **Day 3:** 7; **Day 4:** 9

Answer Key

Page 66
Check students' work and reasoning. 4

Page 67
Check students' work. **Day 1:** 36; **Day 2:** 20; **Day 3:** 57; **Day 4:** 39

Page 68
Check students' work and reasoning. 54

Page 69
Check students' work. **Day 1:** 15 + 10 = 25; **Day 2:** 34 + 30 = 64; **Day 3:** 30 + 8 = 38; **Day 4:** 21 + 10 = 31

Page 70
Check students' work and reasoning. 50

Page 71
Check students' work. **Day 1:** 20; **Day 2:** 30; **Day 3:** 20; **Day 4:** 50

Page 72
Check students' work and reasoning. 70

Page 73
Check students' work. **Day 1:** 46; **Day 2:** 6; **Day 3:** 47; **Day 4:** 99

Page 74
Check students' work and reasoning. 2

Page 75
Day 1–3: Check students' drawings.
Day 4: square

Page 76
Check students' drawings and reasoning. Mark, can

Page 77
Check students' work. **Day 1:** Quan, Trent, Ray; **Day 2:** maple, elm, oak; **Day 3:** Rachel; **Day 4:** green

Page 78
Check students' work and reasoning. second, Answers will vary but may include 4 pencils would be a longer measuring unit than 4 pennies.

Page 79
Check students' work. **Day 1:** 17; **Day 2:** 4; **Day 3:** 5; **Day 4:** 5

Page 80
Check students' work and reasoning. 20

Page 81
Check students' work. **Day 1:** 74; **Day 2:** 38; **Day 3:** 57; **Day 4:** 64

Page 82
Check students' work and reasoning. 7

Page 83
Check students' work. **Day 1:** Bill, Hector; **Day 2:** chickens; **Day 3:** Kaylen, Irene; **Day 4:** tulips

Page 84
Check students' work and reasoning. red

CD-105009 • © Carson-Dellosa

Answer Key

Page 85

Check students' work. **Day 1:** 63; **Day 2:** 65;
Day 3: 32; **Day 4:** 17

Page 86

Check students' work and reasoning. 40

Page 87

Check students' work. **Day 1:** 3; **Day 2:** 2;
Day 3: 4; **Day 4:** is not, 15

Page 88

Check students' work and reasoning. The
chart should have three sections labeled
red, *green*, and *blue*. There should be 8
symbols by red, 5 symbols by green, and 4
symbols by blue. Monique has 17 markers.

Notes

Notes